THE WARREN HOUSE INN
- DARTMOOR -

Tom Greeves & Elisabeth Stanbrook

Bannawell Books
Tavistock

First published in Great Britain 2001
(Quay Publications (Brixham), Tavistock, Devon)
Reprinted 2004

Second Edition 2012 (Bannawell Books, Tavistock, Devon PL19 0DN)
Reprinted 2019
ISBN 978-0-9573361-0-0

British Library Cataloguing in Publication Data
A catalogue record of this title is available from the British Library.

Designed by Kingfisher Print & Design Ltd, Totnes.
Printed by Short Run Press Limited, Exeter.

Front cover: The Warren House Inn in its moorland setting. *Elisabeth Stanbrook.*
Back cover: The fire that has been burning since 1845. *Tom Greeves*

CONTENTS

LIST OF ILLUSTRATIONS

24. The Warren House Inn in the late 1920s (photographer n/k - Stanbrook collection).

25. The Warren House Inn *c*. 1929/30 - (*J. Weston* - courtesy P. Parsons).

26. Mrs Stephens with her daughter Lena (Selina), in the porch of the Warren House Inn, 1920s (*J. Weston* - courtesy P. Parsons).

27. William Stephens (AA patrolman), at the Warren House Inn, 1920s (*J. Weston* – courtesy P. Parsons).

28. Interior of the Warren House Inn, *c*. 1950 (*E. A. Sweetman & Son Ltd* – Stanbrook collection).

29. Moses Bawden's Bungalow/King's Oven Bungalow, east of the Warren House Inn (SX 67538107) in 1976 (*T. Greeves*).

30. 'Silvertop' - Harry Warne at the Warren House Inn, 1920s (*J. Weston* - courtesy P. Parsons).

31. Harry Warne, tin miner at Golden Dagger Mine, late 1920s (*D. Smith?* - courtesy P. Sinclair).

32. Painting of Harry Warne inside the Warren House Inn, *c*. 1935, by R. J. Dymond, with dogs Peter and Paddy (*Charles Worcester & Co.* - Stanbrook collection).

33. The Warren House Inn *c*. 1950, showing Tea Room opposite (*E.A. Sweetman* – Stanbrook collection).

34. The Warren House Inn in deep snow, 1928 (?) (*J. Weston?* - courtesy R. Petherick).

35. Group outside the Warren House Inn *c*. 1944 (photographer n/k - courtesy D. Hurn).

36. Group outside the Warren House Inn with Arthur Hurn third from left, *c*. 1950 (photographer n/k – Greeves collection).

37. Just east of the Warren House Inn in January 1963 - Bawden's Bungalow in background (photographer n/k – Stanbrook collection).

38. Interior of the Warren House Inn and its famous east fireplace, after changes of the mid- 1960s (*K. Ruth* - Stanbrook collection).

39. Interior of the Warren Inn (west fireplace) after changes of the mid-1960s (*K. Ruth* – Greeves collection).

40. Peter and Janet Parsons, August 2001 (*T. Greeves*).

41. The Mid-Devon Hunt meeting outside the Warren House Inn, 20 January 2001 (*T. Greeves*).

42. Peter Parsons behind the bar of the Warren House Inn (*E. Stanbrook*).

INTRODUCTION

The isolated and exposed Warren House Inn at 1425 ft (434m) above sea-level on moorland Dartmoor is justly famed as the highest inn in southern England (south of the Peak District of Derbyshire and Staffordshire)[1], and for the fact that its homely fire is reputed not to have gone out since at least 1845. But it equally deserves attention for the fascinating human history, ranging from the humorous to the tragic, associated with it and its predecessor.

The inn, at Ordnance Survey grid reference SX 674809, was historically in the parish of Lydford, but now lies within the civil parish of Dartmoor Forest. At first sight, such a remote public house might seem strangely out of place. Yet we can be sure that countless thousands of travellers have welcomed the site of a hostelry here, as it is beside an important west-east route that crosses Dartmoor from Tavistock to Moretonhampstead. Its history is also intimately linked with the ancient, distinctive and highly important Dartmoor industries of tinworking and rabbit warrening (from which it takes its name). This is a special place indeed, right on the edge of the ancient Forest of Dartmoor.

Location map

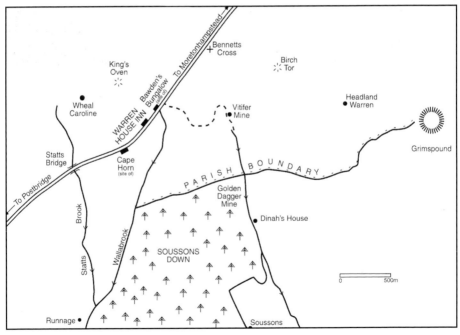

6

King's Oven - prehistoric cairn and boundmark of Forest of Dartmoor   (*T. Greeves*).
PLEASE DO NOT ADD STONES TO THE CAIRN

The First Tourists and King Arthur

There may even have been a traveller's shelter of some kind in the vicinity as long ago as AD 1113 when a group of French monks from Laon in Picardy appear to have visited Dartmoor on a journey from Exeter to Bodmin in Cornwall. The record tells us that they were shown 'King Arthur's Oven' which is very probably to be identified with the prehistoric entrance grave still surviving on the top of Water Hill 425m northwest of the inn. This spot, at 489m, is the highest point to be passed nearby when travelling on the ancient west-east route across Dartmoor, and still bears the name King's Oven. It is a boundary point of the Forest of Dartmoor, noted in the famous 'perambulation' of AD 1240 when it was recorded with the Latin version of its name as 'Furnum Regis'. It is highly likely that the foreign monks would have been shown such a numinous spot associated with the legendary King Arthur.[2]

The Origins of the First Inn

The present Warren House Inn dates from 1845, but it had a predecessor known as New House on the opposite side of the road, for perhaps one hundred years before that time.

The name 'New House' or 'New Inn' is not infrequently given to public houses and other features. For example, from at least 1755 until the mid-19th century there was a New Inn in the centre of the village of Lydford,[3] and from at least the 1820s there was a New Inn at North Bovey.[4] The site of another remote public house (probably of 18th and 19th century date), also called New House, can be seen near Rippon Tor on eastern Dartmoor,[5] at SX 740755.

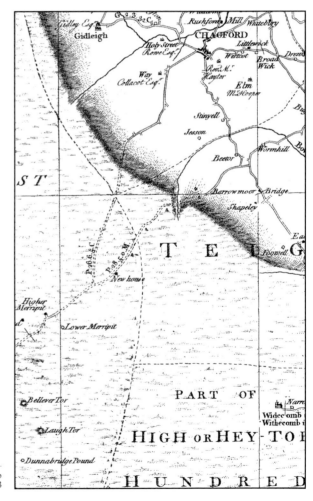

'New house' on Donn's map published in 1765, Sheet 6B

8

Clearly our New House was 'new' at some time, and it may well have been built in about 1760 because this period coincided with a considerable revival in tinworking activity,[6] and the miners would have been glad of a place of lodging and refreshment. Traffic on the road would also have increased considerably from 1772 (the date of the Act of Parliament), during the building, and after completion of, the Moretonhampstead Trust turnpike road,[7] which would have given wheeled vehicles, in place of pack animals, access to central Dartmoor for the first time.

The first definite record of a structure beside the road opposite the present Warren House Inn dates to the mid-18th century when Benjamin Donn surveyed a building called 'New house' which he showed on his map of Devon published in 1765.[8] His fieldwork occupied five summers, probably starting in 1759,[9] so we can be sure that a building was here by 1763 at the very latest.

The non-appearance of New House in a survey of Duchy of Cornwall properties in 1702 which lists thirty-four tenements within the Forest of Dartmoor,[10] suggests that New House was built at some time between 1702 and 1763. Interestingly, in 1737 Richard Wills of Bickington, who was linked with 'Runnage and Walna' from at least 1731, paid 3s rental for 'Three New Takes', with no mention of New House,[11] despite these newtakes (moorland enclosures) almost certainly being the three linked with New House from at least 1786 (see p.13 below). This narrows the probable actual construction of New House to between 1737 and 1763.

But the origins of New House may be very much earlier as many structures with the name element 'new' are actually very old, such as New Bridge over the River Dart near Holne, which is likely to be about 600 years old.

Walna/Warner and a Medieval New House?

Intriguingly, a Dartmoor placename 'New House Wall', probably within the Forest of Dartmoor, is recorded as long ago as 1354-5 in the time of King Edward III.[12] The document refers to a rent of 3d (threepence) being paid 'for a certain wall', which seems an odd element to lease, and it is tempting to suggest this may be a reference to a tenement called Walna, which comprised ground extending southwards from the present Warren House Inn.

The site of a dwelling house for this tenement has not yet been identified. Archaeological fieldwork should be able to resolve this question, but much of the ground to the south of the present Warren House Inn is covered with dense heather which makes exploration difficult. Could New House be on the site of medieval Walna? The orientation of New House (see map, p.17), with its long axis aligned downslope, is suggestive of a medieval site, but its very exposed position would be very surprising for a settlement of that period, as usually the builders were very careful to select a spot protected from the prevailing weather.

The southern boundary of the enclosures associated with New House is defined by the now dry bed of the Birch Tor & Vitifer leat (i.e. mine watercourse) which is thought to date to about 1800 in its present form. However, it may be much earlier in origin as its headweir on the North Teign is shared with a leat known to date to the late 15th century, which led to a mill at Southill near Chagford.[13] In other words, the enclosures below New House should be later than, or contemporary with, the first digging of the Birch Tor & Vitifer leat which was possibly at least 500 years ago. The present-day walls or stone-faced banks of Walna newtake are relatively modern and overlie a medieval complex of enclosure boundaries which could yet reveal the site of a medieval settlement within them. A mine plan of about 1820[14] actually shows two buildings among these medieval boundaries, at approx. SX 67057970, but no trace of a structure can be seen on the surface at this location today, despite its promisingly sheltered position.

'Warner' (a version of Walna) is documented as an 'ancient tenement' as early as 1301-2.[15] The first known user of this land may have been a woman called Clarice, possibly as early as the 13th century, for in 1301-2 accounts record 'decay of rent of half a ferling of land at Walebrook in Dartmoor, which Claricia de Walebrook held, which was in the King's hands for default of a tenant, 2s 6d'.[16] The Wallabrook is the stream south of the Warren House Inn which forms the boundary of the Forest of Dartmoor. 'Walebrook' is among several tenements 'within the Chase' (i.e. Forest) listed under the heading of 'Decay rent' in 1350-1 'for default of tenants',[17] possibly as a result of the Black Death of 1348-9. Between the mid-14th to the mid-15th century rents of 3d are charged in different years to Richard Gold for two acres of land in or between 'Wallabrook land and Runnage' (spellings modernised).[18]

In 1491-2 the Forester records 2d of new rent 'of Richard Canna for a certain parcel of land lying between Stoddesbrook [= Statts Brook] and Walbrook midstreme, so descending by les midstreme of the said water called Walbrook to the Churchway of the said Richard, leading from his tenement towards the Church of Widdicombe'.[19] In 1702 'Rennidge and Warner' were said to be in possession of Richard Braker, and for a time between then and 1731 Michael Mann was lessee.[20]

So, all these interesting records and names of people are linked with the area in question, south of the present Warren House Inn, but whether there was any structure on the site of later New House before the mid-18th century still has to be proved.

Tinworking

There are very few records of tinworking in this area before 1750 but the archaeological evidence is superb.[21] Looking eastwards from the Warren House Inn, extensive gullies can be seen, running roughly east and west. These are all artificial and dug out by miners following tin lodes in the 16th and 17th centuries, and much earlier too. The scale of early working is unparalleled anywhere else in either Devon or Cornwall. As Moses Bawden commented in the early 1900s: 'tens of millions of tons of stuff must have been taken out'.[22] It is a supreme tinworking landscape. Among the few documented early tinworks is 'Boveycombe Hedd' (1522), which is the correct name for the stream marked by the Ordnance Survey as the North Walla Brook a short distance north-east of the Warren House Inn. 'Waterdown Rigge/Rugge' (1522) tinwork must have been sited on Water Hill directly above (north-west) of the Warren House Inn, and 'South Kingesmyth' (1522) tinwork suggests a link with King's Oven itself.[23]

Vitifer Tin Mine *c*. 1911 (detail from *Chapman & Son* 11954 - Greeves collection)

New House was actually a key focus of tin mining activity in the late 18th century, for in May 1788 tin to the value of £667 was sold from 'a small piece of ground part of the Forest of Dartmoor and situated near a house known by the name of the New House - that as well previous to such sale as subsequent to it considerable quantities of Tin have been carried off from the said spot and made merchantable...by persons of opulence residing in London'.[24]

From the mid-18th century the most important mines were those of Vitifer, Birch Tor and Golden Dagger, on the south side of the road, and Wheal Caroline and New Vitifer Consols to the north. Several hundred men and boys were employed in peak years. The last commercial mine (Golden Dagger) closed in November 1930,[25] though some of the buildings remained occupied until the Second World War.

Rabbit Warrening

A commercial rabbit warren once existed immediately south of the site of New House. The warren contains the indistinct remains of at least two characteristic 'vermin traps' (at SX 67378032 and SX 67438065), which are similar to those at other Dartmoor warrens of the 17th or 18th century. At some time the warren was apparently known as 'New House Warren'.[26]

Adjoining this warren, on the east side of the Wallabrook, was Headland Warren, known also as Mead's or Roberts Warren, after the names of the occupiers. In Gough's late-18th century edition of Camden's Britannia it is stated that 'On great part of the old tin mine [Vitifer] there is a warren, which supplies Exeter with abundance of rabbits'.[27] On Friday 6 May 1796, Charles Hatchett passed along the road and, although his main interest was in the tin mine, he noted that 'near the mine is a rabbit warren which lets at £80 per ann.'.[28] The Revd John Swete passed by in 1795 and 1797 and described the scene as follows: 'On my approach to the turnpike [from Chagford], I found myself surrounded by innumerable Rabbits, and recognizing a house or two by the way side discover'd that I was at Mead's Warren. To it there was no fence but a few stones piled on one another, and ranged in a certain line, evidently serving to ascertain its limits than to preclude the Rabbits from roving: indeed on the dry hill beyond this barrier or boundary they appeared to me to be as numerous, as they were within the restricted line...nothing could well be more wild and rugged than this spot...'.[29] Early in 1803 (probably March) Eric Svedenstierna, a Swede, also used this route, noting 'one or two miserable huts' but 'no sign of a living being...apart from rabbits, which grub up and undermine the soil everywhere'.[30] Although observing buildings, none of these travellers mentioned New House itself. By 1817 this area was described as 'Roberts Warren' in which 'Videford Tin Mine' was located.[31]

Recollecting the early 20th century, Frank Hodge remembered 'there was hundreds and thousands of rabbits there in they days'.[32]

A Dartmoor rabbit trapper
(*Chapman & Son* - Greeves collection)

NEW HOUSE AND THE MORETON INN
c.1760 - 1845

The earliest known lessee of New House was William Tapper who held it in 1786. He paid his rental of three shillings for land described as 'including Newhouse 3 Newtakes', thus implying that New House was sited within the enclosures previously leased to Richard Wills in 1737 (see above, p.9).[33]

References to 'New Inn' among 'victuallers recognizances' between 1801 and 1812 are likely to refer to the inn of that name in Lydford village rather than New House, as the personal names have no known connection with moorland Dartmoor.[34] Our site is marked as New House on maps published in 1812, 1816, 1822, 1825, 1829, and in 1830.[35]

Parish and other records fill in some detail of those who lived at New House in the early years of the 19th century, when it was sometimes known as the Moreton Inn (also spelt Mooreton/Mortin/Mooron/Moorton).

Robert Browning was the licensee of the Moreton Inn from 1815 -1823.[36] Two-year-old Mary 'Brining' [i.e. Browning] of New House was buried at Widecombe on 24 February 1815.[37] On 3 September 1820, Mary Browning aged 39 of New House, Lydford, was buried at Widecombe.[38] From 1824-1826 James Jenkin took over as licensee of the Moreton Inn.[39]

William Henry Tamblyn, the son of Marianne and John, a miner of New House, was baptised at Lydford on 24 April 1825.[40] From 1827-8 William Honey (also spelt Huns) was innkeeper of the Moreton Inn.[41] On 14 November 1830 James Pope, son of William, a miner, and Jane his wife of 'New-house, Lydford' was baptised at Widecombe.[42] Both Brownings and Popes were mining families and lodged at New House. Within a few years (by 1838) the Popes had moved to Stamps Cottage, Manaton[43] which was on the site of the mine more commonly known as Golden Dagger, nearly one mile to the south-east.

John Churcher (?) aged 38 and Henry Bawden aged 27, both of 'Newhouse', were buried at Lydford in January 1838 and March 1839 respectively.[44]

The First Eyewitness

The earliest surviving eyewitness account of New House dates to 27 July 1831 when Mr Bray (1778-1857) stopped there on 'an extremely hot day' with his wife Anna Eliza. He was scornful of the premises, discovering there was not even room in the stable for their horses as it was 'full of turf ' (i.e. peat). However, he reveals several very interesting pieces of information. He noted that the building was 'formerly an inn' and that the woman he spoke to was 'a representative' of the former landlady, and had lived there 'no more than two years'. She may in fact have been Jane Pope. He had been told by the farmer at Beardown, near Two Bridges, a man called Hannaford, that 'it was one of the oldest houses on the moor'. Bray also indicated that it had seen 'better days'. He observed that the house was 'surrounded by a warren' and recalled a sign he had seen when a boy (i.e. in the 1780s or early 1790s), with the verses

Here is cider and beer,
Your hearts for to cheer.
If you want meat
To make up a treat,
There are rabbits to eat.[45]

Doubt has been cast on the accuracy of his memory as a building at Headland Warren, just over a mile to the east, apparently had a similar sign on its door when it once served as a hostelry for miners,[46] but it is not impossible that one was borrowed from the other.

The Romantic Packhorse Driver

Bray also recounted a romantic story linked to New House, of a 'pack-horse driver', or carrier, whose singing prowess in a public house on St David's Hill, Exeter (probably the Pack Horse Inn, noted in *Pigot's Directory* of 1830, as Bray remarks that the public house in question was 'a pretty general rendezvous' for persons of this description), had won the heart of a clergyman's daughter. The couple were married and set up home at New House. Carriers between Exeter and Moretonhampstead in 1830 included Robert Wills, Frost and Kerslake,[47] and one of these may well have been the carrier in question. It may be significant that a John Frost, a publican of Okehampton, and another John Frost, a wheelwright of Moretonhampstead, were among a group of eleven persons who assigned shares in Wheal Caroline tin mine (only about 500m west of New House) to Thomas and Samuel Honichurch in May 1825.[48]

The Salted Corpse

Perhaps the most famous story alleged to be associated with New House is that concerning a traveller who, at some time before 1832, and probably in the 18th century, was given a room for the night by an old woman and her son, in severe wintry conditions. A chest inside the room attracted his attention and, unable to sleep, his curiosity got the better of him. He opened it to find, to his horror, a corpse inside. In fear for his own life he spent a sleepless and cold night, but endured until the morning when, at a hearty breakfast, he summoned up courage to ask for an explanation. 'Bless your heart, your honour', said the old woman's son,' 'tis nothing at all, 'tis only fayther!...the snaw being so thick, and making the roads so cledgey-like, when old fayther died, two weeks agon, we couldn't carry un to Tavistock to bury un; and so mother put un in the old box, and salted un in: mother's a fine hand at salting un in'.[49]

It is not absolutely proven that this event took place at New House, as the earliest version of the story only mentions a 'cottage' and an 'old outhouse', and not specifically an inn.[50] However, it was substantial enough to have an upstairs chamber, and has been generally associated with New House for well over one hundred years. It is a highly evocative tale, based on what would undoubtedly have been a genuine practice on remote and wintry Dartmoor.

Another version of the same story is recorded by Theo Brown in her 'Tales of a Dartmoor Village', in which the daughter reaches Widecombe and reports the death to the vicar. When he is told that the death occurred six weeks earlier, the vicar is aghast, but the girl reassures him that there is no need for haste, as 'We'd just killed the pig, and we was saltin' 'un down, so mother - 'er put father in too' ![51]

Jonas Coaker

Jonas Coaker first occupied the 'Warreners Inn' in 1834.[52] The Lydford tithe apportionment of 1839[53] records Jonas Coaker as the occupier of 'New House and Warren' including 'New House Inn and Garden' / 'Inn House and Garden', with two arable plots plus one of pasture, totalling 2 acres 1 rood 5 poles. In 1841, the first detailed census recorded Jonas Coaker, aged 40, his wife Susan [née Austin] aged 30, and their three daughters Elizabeth, Ann and Jane aged 9, 4 and 1 respectively, all in residence at New House. In 1843 a traveller from Moretonhampstead noted the inn as 'the first sign of human habitation' on the open moor, and described it as 'a stone cot surrounded by a low wall and a peat stack; a board suspended

Jonas Coaker (1801-1890) - from Wright, 1896, 99

15

nearest the road-side proclaims to the way-worn traveller that Jonas Coaker is a licensed victualler; his wife is the mother of four really fine and truly clean children, whom she assured us she was bringing up on the moor, and they certainly did credit to their pasture.' [54] The youngest child was George, born that year.[55]

Jonas Coaker (1801-1890) was a well-known character of 19th-century Dartmoor having a variety of occupations and living to the considerable age of 89. He was self-styled 'The Dartmoor Poet', and several of his verses have survived.[56] Life as a publican among tough and sometimes unruly miners was not easy. Jonas Coaker was once forced to abandon the pub and to 'hidey-peep' on the moor while the miners helped themselves to his ale.[57] In another incident, a miner was killed in a fight. His assailant received only three weeks in prison, thanks in part to the evidence of Jonas Coaker who helped establish 'gross provocation'.[58] Jonas Coaker relinquished his tenancy on the inn in 1845,[59] but it is not unlikely that he was present at the transition from one side of the road to the other.

The Field Remains

Dated February 1840, a survey of a proposed railway line from Plymouth to Exeter, passing New House by means of an inclined plane, shows the first detailed record of the layout of the site, which is still recognisable today on the south side of the road. The site was described as 'Public House with Outhouses'. Three fields between the road and the mine leat contained one sizeable rectangular building aligned downslope, with its upper gable end more or less on the road edge itself. A small garden plot and/or building was shown immediately west of the house. Below the mine leat was a Rabbit Warren, on waste land. The lessee of the Duchy of Cornwall was recorded as John Wills; the actual occupier as Jonas Coaker.[60]

Today the small fields associated with New House can still be seen opposite the Warren House Inn. Of the house itself virtually nothing remains. Its location was at the east end of concrete foundations (for pre-War stables), and very faint traces of a rectangular structure aligned downslope can be seen at the edge of the field. It seems likely that the top end of the building was close to the modern road, and then extended about 14.5m downslope, on a rough NW-SE axis, to a modern cross wall which may represent the lower end of the structure. Its maximum internal width would have been about 4m. The site of its porch, on its west side, is now obscured by the concrete platform.

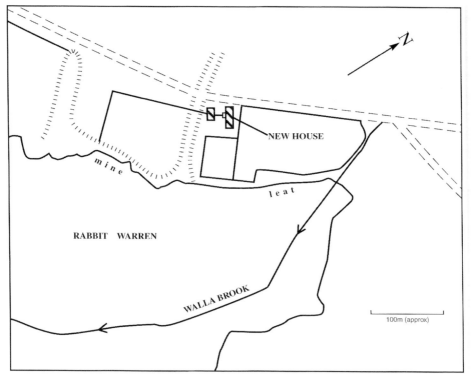

NEW HOUSE

mine

leat

RABBIT   WARREN

WALLA BROOK

100m (approx)

Plan of New House 1840 (after DRO/DP 148)

1845 - THE INN MOVES

Of special interest as far as the history of the present Warren House Inn is concerned is that Bray was told by his female informant that within the past two years (i.e. in about 1830) a 'pedlar' had advised her to pull down New House, because of its poor state of repair, and rebuild it on the other side of the road, 'where a foundation for a similar purpose had been already laid, or at least the ground dug out for it... in a line with the corner of their field near the mire'.[61]

Despite the dilapidated state of New House at the time of Mr and Mrs Bray's visit in 1831, it was not until 1845 that John Wills built a replacement inn on the opposite side of the road. Work was completed by September, and a neatly inscribed slate plaque with a curiously precise date is set into the external eastern gable wall and reads 'I.Wills, Sept[r]. 18, 1845'.

Slate plaque of 1845 built into the east gable wall of Warren House Inn (*T. Greeves*).

18

It is from this date that the story of the peat fire never having gone out can be attributed. Apparently, smouldering peat from the New House fire was carried across the road and placed in the new fireplace of the Warren House Inn, on the right as one enters the premises today. It has been suggested that a 'Lias' (Elias) Warne lit the original fire.[62] Tradition maintains it has burned continuously since September 1845, with the type of fuel changing from peat to a mixture of peat (vags) and wood, and now wood alone.

Baring-Gould in his *Dartmoor Idylls* claims that the old inn was burnt down, but no supporting evidence for this has yet come to light, nor is there evidence to support his story that Jonas Coaker built the new inn, or that there was a surprise new payment of rent to the Duchy of Cornwall when the Warren House Inn had been completed.[63]

In Rowe's *Perambulation of Dartmoor*, which was published in 1848, the inn was described as 'small' but where 'a carriage can be put up' for those travellers wishing to visit Grimspound, a prehistoric enclosure some two miles distant.[64]

In February 1850 the national weekly *Mining Journal* recorded an incident at the 'New House Inn' involving tin miners. The 'most disgraceful affair' occurred, allegedly, on Saturday 27 January at the inn 'where the miners went to divide their pay and to drink. In the evening a most brutal fight took place, in which the agent [i.e. Capt. Dunstan, the mine captain], much to his disgrace, instead of using his authority to quell the disturbance, encouraged the combatants, by calling out "good boys", "at 'em again," and other such expressions of approbation at the sight'. The correspondent was not surprised that so little tin ore was being produced as it was the third or fourth time that he had heard of similar quarrels, and four days later (31 January) the men involved in the fight had still not returned to work.

This account was hotly disputed by Capt. Richard Dunstan of Birch Tor in a letter dated 5 February. He claimed that the fight did not involve Vitifer men, and that the only reason small quantities of tin had been produced was due to the severity of the weather. A further very interesting comment was made by Joseph Elliot Square, Secretary of Birch Tor & Vitifer Mines, in the *Mining Journal* of 16 February: 'The Inn is not only a public house, but the only market for butchers' meat in the locality (the centre of Dartmoor). This accounts for the presence of Capt. Dunstan there, he having been a teetotaller for many years.'[65]

The Warnes

On John Wills's death in 1850, his son, also called John, successfully applied to the Duchy to take over the lease of the 'Public House called the Warreners Inn... recently erected by him', plus Walna and Runnage, and this was granted in October 1851.[66] In the meantime, by 1850, Joseph Warne, originally from Sampford Spiney, had become the innkeeper of the 'Moreton Inn' and occupier of the rabbit warren.[67] With him lived his wife, Elizabeth, and their children. Lodgers were taken in, which must have helped supplement their income, and in 1851 the Census Return shows a tin miner, William Jilberts aged 29 from Cornwall, and an agricultural labourer, Thomas Wreford, as residing there.

At this time the inn was often visited by an important mining figure, Capt. John Palk (or Paull), who was also known as 'Quaker Palk'. Capt. Palk (*c.* 1793-1853) had been for years much involved with Dartmoor mines, especially nearby Vitifer and Birch Tor. Baring-Gould relates how, on one occasion in the Warren Inn, despite being 'a sturdy teetotaller' and given to lecturing on total abstinence, 'Captain Palk, in helping himself to brandy, put his hand round the glass, to hide the quantity he poured in, but when the brown liquid rose above his palm, Mr Pearce [his companion] stared and uttered an exclamation, "Ah, John Pearce," said Palk, "I tell thee that the Warren Inn is the highest public-house in all England, and one must live up to one's elevation." ' This incident occurred when Mr Warne was the publican.[68]

In 1855, tragedy struck the Warne family with the death of their son, Joseph, at the young age of 13. He was buried at Widecombe on 21 February.[69] The Warnes left the inn not long afterwards, and William Jinnings is recorded as innkeeper in 1857.[70]

Besides being a collecting point for meat, the Warren House Inn appears to have been used as a useful location for the delivery of other goods from one part of the moor to another. For example, in 1858, a Mr Bray from Okehampton was asked by Charles Barrington, the Duchy Steward, whether he had any seedlings from forest trees, and at what price per 1,000 he could deliver them to the inn for collection.[71] There was obviously a favourable response because, sixteen months later, Mr Bray was still delivering there.[72]

Travellers of all sorts stopped for rest and refreshment. One included a naive farmer who was persuaded by a crafty man called Debben to buy some 'wethers', i.e. sheep, and, having made the bargain, was told where he could find them on the moor, nearly three miles north of Postbridge. He did find 'wethers' there but they turned out to be the stones of two prehistoric circles known as 'The Grey Wethers' to this day.[73]

William Jinnings did not stay long at the inn, for by 1861 he had been replaced by William Maddock, aged 24, who also ran the rabbit warren on the inn's land.[74] Duchy records reveal that the inn and Walna newtake were currently 'rated' at £13.[75] By May 1863, the Warne family had returned to the 'Rabbit's Warren' inn.[76] As well as working

Grey Wethers
prehistoric stone circles
(*Chapman & Son -*
Stanbrook collection)

as innkeeper, Joseph, together with his son George, was employed as a miner, presumably at the nearby tin mines of Birch Tor, Golden Dagger or Vitifer.[77] The inn, sometimes still known as the Moreton Inn,[78] was much frequented by tin miners, and locals were known to complain that they could not get into the premises because it was packed with these workers.[79]

A future miner was born in the Warren House Inn on 14 May 1867. He was Elias Tucker (son of another Elias, a skilled miner) and was the first child to be christened at Postbridge Church (his infant sibling Charles of 'Newhouse' was buried at Widecombe on 9 December 1867[80]). Growing up on the moor, he became interested in its minerals, and went into the mining industry in Cumberland. He later returned to Chagford and, after marrying, moved to India where he became Captain of a gold mine. Later years saw him in Spain, the Canary Islands and back to Kent in England. He then moved to Newton Abbot and was instrumental in the opening of Pepperdon iron mine. He visited Dartmoor regularly until his death in 1949 aged 82.[81] Another miner, Samuel Oldridge, who in November 1858 had married Jane, the daughter of Joseph and Elizabeth Warne, was residing at 'New House, Chagford' in October 1867, when granted a licence of a tin sett nearby.[82]

At 4 a.m. on 24 August 1873 any occupants of the inn would have been rudely awoken by the 23rd Highland Regiment, with pipes and drums, passing by on their way to join several thousand other troops camped on Merripit Hill, one mile to the west, as part of large-scale military manoeuvres.[83]

James (Jim) Hannaford (c. 1825 -1899) of Headland Warren had a lucky escape one night when walking home from the Warren Inn in about 1874. Passing too close to an air shaft near Hamlyn's Gully, only about half a mile from the inn, the ground gave way and he fell about 14ft (4.3m) into the blackness, to be caught on some timbers, with a dripping cavity below. His collie dog stayed with him at the shaft all night, and eventually guided searchers to the plight of his master the next day. Jim Hannaford was safely rescued but was crippled by the experience. However, he never forgot how his dog saved his life.[84]

James (Jim) Hannaford (second from left) + family at Headland Warren c. 1895. (photographer n/k - courtesy A. Mortimore)

Crossing records a tale of a couple from Widecombe who had gone to 'Newhouse' in connection with a christening, but who were forced to stay there for a week, on account of snow![85]

The pub was still often known by the name of its predecessor across the road - for example, in February 1869 J. Daynty of Holmbush Mine, Stoke Climsland, wrote to the Duchy of Cornwall asking for the grant of a mine sett 'West of the New House Inn',[86] and even the Duchy of Cornwall referred to it as 'New House Inn" in February 1870.[87] In February 1875 Moses Bawden recorded, 'I have recently purchased the Cottages erected by Mr Bayly and others near New House'.[88] Murray's classic *A Handbook for Travellers in Devonshire* was still calling it 'New House' in its revised tenth edition of 1887.[89] Among the older generation on Dartmoor the name lingered well into the 20th century - Fred Willcocks, who was born at Middle Cator in 1913, recalled that 'all the old people' knew it as New House when he was young.[90]

Joseph Warne's death in December 1882 at the age of 78[91] ended that family's long occupation of the Warren House Inn, and the Hext family succeeded them.

Thomas and Elizabeth Hext

Thomas and Elizabeth Hext were to stay at the Warren House Inn for nearly forty years. It is Tommy Hext (born at Hartyland, Postbridge in about 1846), whose father James had worked as a shepherd at Runnage,[92] who made an impression on many people. He was often described as having a long beard, which he was fond of stroking, and stood about 6ft 2in tall. He is also said to have worked as a tin miner.[93] However, it was Elizabeth (born in about 1849) whom Duchy records reveal as apparently having responsibility for the place, being named as tenant instead of Tommy. In March 1897 Mr Hext was paid £1.00 by the Duchy of Cornwall for filling in old mine shafts on Bush Down.[94]

In 1898, John Wills II died and his son, another John (III), living at Lenda in Ilsington, took over the lease, undertaking a few minor repairs to the inn, although the Hexts remained in occupancy as landlords.[95]

Tommy Hext (?) in porch of Warren House Inn *c.* 1900 - note misspelling of 'SPIRITS'!
(photographer n/k - courtesy A. Mortimore)

Horse-drawn carriage outside the Warren House Inn *c.* 1900   (photographer n/k - Greeves collection)

The bulk drink stocked by the Hexts was beer or cider, all kept out in the back yard. Mrs Hext would take the order and 'shuffle out' to fetch it.[96] Sometimes supplies ran low and barrels had to be bought hastily from Chagford to keep the customers happy! Tommy Hext was apparently 'renowned for diluting the beer with water' in the summer months, but was fond of a drink himself and, after visits to relatives, would often be laid on his horse which would find its own way back to the inn.[97]

Interviewed in the 1970s, Frank Hodge, recalling the mining days before the First World War, said, 'there's been some rare fun up there!'

Cape Horn'/West Bungalow *c.* 1912. Miners' accommodation SX 6722 8070, on the opposite side of the road to the Warren House Inn, towards Postbndge (*Chapman & Son* 11726 - Greeves collection)

He described the inn as 'a big bare room, there wasn't a picture or anything in it, and you sat in the window, a great long seat'. Of the peat fire he said, 'That fire was always in, always in', and the men used to heat their quart (two pints) of ale in a funnel standing in the fire.[98] Beer was 2½d a pint, an ounce of tobacco 3½d, and port and lemon 2½d.[99] An old man called Clark, a miner, always used to sit in one corner.[100]

As before, the main customers of the inn comprised tin miners from Birch Tor, Golden Dagger and Vitifer mines, which attracted men from all quarters of the moor. Miners from South Zeal would stop at the inn on their way to the Postbridge mines on a Monday. They had a prodigious capacity for drink, and might consume up to sixteen pints of beer each. They could buy four or five pints for one shilling (5p). They earned up to about 24 shillings (£1.20) a week.[101] On one occasion, while enjoying their pints before work, there was such a heavy fall of snow that a group of men had to stay there the whole day![102]

Some of the miners lodged at the inn itself. One, John Hellier (1854-1927), was born at the Drewe Arms, Drewsteignton, and would walk over from Sticklepath and lodge at the inn for the week. He told his grandson that, while staying there, the miners' damp clothes would sometimes freeze stiff overnight.[103] At the time of the census of 1891 Albert Pearce, a single man aged 25, born in Buckfastleigh and working as a tin miner, was listed as a 'Boarder'.[104] In 1901 Evalina Parr, the 20-year-old niece of Tommy and Elizabeth Hext, was also living at the inn.[105]

The Warren House Inn iced up in wintry weather, 1920s (*J. Weston* ? - Stanbrook collection)

The Postbridge mines attracted labour from far and wide, and it was not unusual for Welshmen or Scotsmen to be employed, along with casual labour from men travelling on the road. This interesting mixture of cultures used to lead to a great many quarrels and fights at the Warren House Inn because the men were sometimes barely able to understand each other. John Leaman, who was born in 1889, remembered his father saying the noise was 'as if a pig were being killed up there sometimes'.[106] On other occasions, Cornish miners would wrestle outside the inn.[107] Fortunately, it seemed the Duchy turned a blind eye or did not get to hear of these events which might have jeopardised Mrs Hext's tenancy. Despite these difficulties, in 1904 it was said that Mrs Hext 'always kept the house respectable and well conducted'.[108]

A potentially serious incident occurred in the early 1900s when Gertrude Chudley, then a teenager, was employed to look after a child at Vitifer Mine. When returning from church at Postbridge at dusk one day, she spotted what she thought was a large dog beside the road, but it turned out to be a man who chased her. Fortunately she was too quick for him and got away. That very evening the same man threatened a miner with a piece of wood. Some days later the man rashly entered the Warren House Inn and drank a pint of beer belonging to Harry 'Silvertop' Warne. The miners meted out their own justice by grabbing the man, taking him outside and a short way down the hillslope, where they threw him into the mine leat, washing him up and down several times. They threw his hat after him and the man was never seen again in the area.[109] Gertrude Chudley's sister Bessie was working at the Warren House Inn in 1911, when she was aged twenty-one, and was courted by one of the miners. Also boarding at the inn was a labourer called Stephen Clark, aged thirty-five, who had been born in Lustleigh. [110]

Visitors in a variety of horse-drawn conveyances would stop at the inn, as did various traders. A baker from the Poundsgate area delivered bread to Vitifer Mine by cart. He often called at the Warren House Inn and would get rather inebriated. On the way down to the mine his cart sometimes tipped up, depositing loaves in the stream.[111]

In 1905 a boy was born in a caravan near the Warren House Inn to the lover of a man - Augustus John - who was to earn a national reputation as an artist. The boy was called Pyramus and his mother was Dorelia McNeill. In her pregnancy, Mr and Mrs Hext kept a kindly eye on her and ensured visits from a doctor and nurse. Augustus John who, with his wife Ida, joined Dorelia soon after the birth, referred to the Hexts as 'two primitives'. This may not have been intended unkindly, as he was clearly attached to the Warren House Inn where he described how, 'A peat fire warmed the plain flagged kitchen, which was provided with settles'. Many years later he visited it again and wrote of changes to it disparagingly in his autobiography which was published in 1952: 'the flags have been disguised under cheerful linoleum from Tottenham Court Road. Dainty teas are now served on 'plastic' tables, and creaky wicker-work chairs have taken the place of the settles. A few choice advertisements provided gratuitously by benevolent business firms complete the decor'[112], though it seems more likely that he was in fact describing the pre-Second World War tea-rooms across the road from the inn itself. Augustus John's caravan is likely to have been sited near Statts Bridge, some 850m south-west of the inn.[113]

An Inland Revenue survey of about 1910, describes the Warren House Inn as being in a poor state of repair. It reveals the accommodation as comprising a sitting room, taproom, kitchen and cellar on the ground floor, with four bedrooms on the first floor. A WC (water closet lavatory) was in the yard.[114] There was general consideration given to enlarging and improving the inn. Plans were discussed to re-roof the property and add two ground floor rooms plus three or four rooms upstairs, with a bathroom, water supply and 'sanitary accommodation'. A small coach or motor house was considered, with an estimated cost of £400. None of these improvements was carried out.

The Hexts renegotiated their tenancy from Michaelmas 1911 with the Duchy, with the clause that 'the Tenancy will be determined at three months notice if complaints are received from the Manager of Golden Dagger or Birch Tor Mines and justified on account of the Miners being incapacitated by drink sold at the Inn'.[115]

By the beginning of 1912, the Warren House Inn had fallen into a very bad state of repair with rain penetrating the windows and covering the floors of the front rooms! Mrs Hext requested repairs, with an enlargement of the premises to be undertaken at the same time. By the end of 1912, neither had been done, and a desperate Mrs Hext wrote to the Duchy saying, 'we are in a terrible state'. This letter was in vain as by May 1913, Mrs Hext's further letter reveals: '... the windows are rotten. I am afraid to have the glass cleaned for fear it would drop out... You never saw such a place to live in the rain [has] been coming in all over the place. I had to have my bed remove[d] all about the room while I was in bed.... The Dr has ordered me off the Moor for a change.' This did prompt a response and the Duchy agreed to the repairs and also the request for enlargement. Architects Richardson & Gill drew up plans which would have cost £928 6s 11d to implement. Mrs Hext felt this was too much, so the plans were modified to £500. Work on the repairs was authorised and this was undertaken by Messrs Stone & Sons of Chagford.[116]

The Warren House Inn c.1911 (*Chapman & Son* 11741 - Greeves collection)

Bennetts Cross   (*E. Stanbrook*)

In the meantime, Mr C. G. Moor, the Technical Advisor at Golden Dagger Mine, complained to the Duchy about drunken miners at the inn. Upon investigation, it turned out that Mrs Hext had refused to serve one miner after trouble he and a colleague had caused. Both had now left the neighbourhood. Fortunately, a local policeman was able to assure the Duchy that there was never any trouble at the inn during his visits![116] Mrs Vera Cole (b. 1906) recalled that a miner called 'Bill Mac' once got drunk at the inn and attacked the medieval granite of Bennetts Cross, thinking it was a person, and injured his hands quite badly.[118]

In February 1914 repairs to the inn were finished. Despite these, rain still came inside the inn. To make matters worse, visitors were complaining about the drain leading out from the stable which was spilling its contents in the road and attracting flies. The smell was not appreciated either!

About the time of the First World War, Mrs Polly Warne, wife of tin miner Harry Warne, used to do washing for Mrs Hext. She carried clothes to and from a timber bungalow in which the family then lived at Vitifer Mine, a distance of about half a mile.[119]

John Wills III died in 1915 and his daughters Annie and Clara became manorial tenants in September 1917, but sold their interest in Runnage and Walna (which included the Warren House Inn) to the Duchy of Cornwall for £1,825 on 12 February 1918, thus ending that family's long connection with the area.[120]

W.T. Stephens, landlord, 1920s (*J. Weston* - courtesy P. Parsons)

The Stephens Family

William ('Billy Buck') Toop Stephens, from Horrabridge, who had worked as a carpenter at Vitifer Mine,[121] and at Princetown, took over the tenancy of the Warren House Inn in about 1921. The tenancy included a bungalow. Recent improvements carried out had led to an increase in trade, and Mr Stephens, who lived there with his wife Mary, two sons William and Alfred, and daughter Lena (Selina), now wanted extra bedroom accommodation. A third son, Charlie, lived elsewhere. Architects Richardson & Gill, who were working on the Temperance Hotel in Postbridge and Prince Hall near Two Bridges, were employed to draw up plans in February 1922. Three months later, the possibility of an AA (Automobile Association) box sited at the inn was under discussion. By the end of 1923, Mr Stephens had bought a motor car and was asking the Duchy for a garage plus a cow house, which would cost £500.[122]

In 1924, the plans for enlargement were still being considered, with Mr Stephens now wanting a lounge or private sitting room, seven bedrooms, and a room 30ft by 15ft, big enough to accommodate a char-a-banc party. 'He demurs to the ladies having to go upstairs as some of those calling are hardly entitled to be so designated as they would require a detective'. He also requested a lean-to on the Postbridge side to be extended into a garage.[123]

The Warren House Inn in the 1920s (*J. Weston* - courtesy P. Parsons)

The Warren House Inn
from the east, 1920s
(*J. Weston -*
courtesy P. Parsons)

Warren House Inn
from the west, 1920s,
with Charlie Stephens
(*J. Weston* - courtesy
P. Parsons)

A well-to-do group
outside the Warren
House Inn, 1920s
(*J. Weston* - courtesy
P. Parsons)

The Postbridge miners continued their drinking at the inn. A former miner remembered in the mid-1920s being sent to the inn to fetch bottles of beer in a sack for the men at Golden Dagger at dinner time while the boss was away![124] Mr Austin Irish (b. 1907) remembered walking to the inn from Grendon Farm (two miles to the south) in the late 1920s, with his two brothers and a girl called Pam who lived near Challacombe. They followed a well-trodden path across Soussons Down and through the mine workings, but carried no lantern with them. He recollected Mr Stephens as a 'strict old fellow', with no sense of humour, though some knew him by the name of 'Uncle Tom Cobleigh'.[125]

In the late 1920s a small group of men from Whiddon Down lodged at the Warren House Inn, and then walked daily from there to Broadamarsh on the East Dart, a distance of 3½ miles as the crow flies, to work sinking trial pits for a prospective chinaclay works. They included Freddy Hall and Sid 'Snail' Snell, who was said to have a continually dripping nose![126]

Interior of the Warren
House Inn bar, 1920s -
W. Stephens (r.)
talking with Austin
Weston (*J. Weston* –
courtesy P. Parsons)

Crowds outside the Warren House Inn, expecting the Prince of Wales (later King Edward VIII) to pass, 1920s (*J. Weston* - courtesy P. Parsons)

The Warren House Inn in the late 1920s (photographer n/k - Stanbrook collection)

Dances were also held regularly in a hut opposite the inn. They were popular occasions with a band, and attended by miners and Postbridge people.[127]

Tourists were becoming more frequent, and a poem titled 'The Warren House Inn' written by one F. Johnson, was printed on the back of a postcard when the Stephenses were there, and captures something of the period:

The Warren House Inn, a famous old Inn,
On the Hills of Old Dartymoor;
The Hostess, Mrs Stephens by name, is at
The ever open door.
The people are swarming to a smile that is warming,
And a heart that is full of good cheer;
If you've travelled a mile and would rest awhile,
She'll supply you with good English beer.

The chars-a bancs stays - well I mean the Greys;
In fact I am told they must stop.
As they come o'er the hill their hearts give a thrill,
They can hear the corks popping and pop
Out of the car and into the bar,
Where they are greeted by Lena;
If she smiles your way you'll be happy this day -
I know, because I have seen her.

So here's good luck to the Warren House Inn
With its good Demshur cream and cider.
May the fame of the old house. North, South, East or West,
Ever get wider and wider.
And when the storm crashes on the Moor o'er the night
And the thunder creates such a din,
I'll sup the good ale and smoke the good pipe
At peace in the Warren House Inn.

But tragedy was to strike. Around 7 p.m. one evening in late March 1929, William Stephens shot himself in the bar, dying instantly, at the age of 58.[128] Word about this swiftly travelled the neighbourhood and the Duchy started receiving offers from outside parties to take over the tenancy of the inn. But on 27 March, at the Tavistock Petty Sessions, Mary Stephens was granted a licence to sell intoxicating liquors at the Warren House Inn until 30 April 1930.[129]

Mrs Stephens carried on at the inn, no doubt with help from her children, William (Bill), Lena and Alfred, but in January 1930, tragedy struck again, when William, an AA patrolman, was killed (aged thirty-three) in a sidecar accident at Dartmeet (Princetown side).[130] Only four years later his brother Alfred was also killed in a motorcycle accident. Donald Smith, who was the young manager of Golden Dagger Mine until November 1930, was a friend and contemporary of Alfred's and recalled how they used to race each other on their motorcycles to and from Tavistock.[131]

The Warren House Inn *c.* 1929/30 - (*J. Weston* - courtesy P. Parsons)

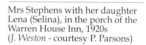

Mrs Stephens with her daughter Lena (Selina), in the porch of the Warren House Inn, 1920s
(*J. Weston* - courtesy P. Parsons)

William Stephens (AA patrolman), at the Warren House Inn, 1920s
(*J. Weston* – courtesy P. Parsons)

On medical grounds, in February 1930, Mrs Stephens decided to leave. This prompted the Duchy to look for a new tenant, and Mr Arthur Hurn of South Hessary House, Princetown, was chosen to take over the inn and Walna on 29 September 1930 for 14 years at a rent of £14 p.a.[132]

However, all did not go smoothly. Mrs Stephens refused to make plans to vacate the premises. She had wanted a man from Totnes to take over the tenancy, and was demanding a valuation on two bungalows which were to be sold together with her furniture. In the meantime, Mr Hurn was making enquiries about sinking tanks from which to sell petrol at the inn. He also applied to erect four loose boxes at about £180. He then purchased one of the huts which was a Tea Room. Mrs Stephens finally vacated the inn and Arthur and Elsie Hurn and family were able to move into their new home later in the year.[133]

The Hurn Family

Mr Arthur James Hurn had been at Oxford with the Prince of Wales and they had remained friends. In 1917, he and his family moved from Windsor Castle to South Hessary House, Princetown, where he was responsible for the Prince of Wales's horses at Tor Royal. Arthur Hurn's son, David, attended Princetown School and then went on to attend Christ's Hospital School (Bluecoats) in 1926; he remembers the long rail journey from Princetown. There were two other children, Peter and Joan.

Of the interior of the inn, David Hurn remembered that, on entering the premises, the bar was on the right and the family sitting room on the left. Another door straight ahead, which could be locked, led to the stairs. The Hurns later added a bathroom downstairs. The bar was lit by two Aladdin lamps, and on the back of the door was a 'ring board'. The fire was still fuelled by peat which was dug on Water Hill above the inn, and also near Vitifer Mine. Once cut, the peat would be brought back on galvanised sheeting pulled by a pony. Hamlyn Parsons, a post-War Dartmoor writer of repute, recalled that 'the smell of the smouldering peat "Vags" is delightful when wafted down the hill on a chilly evening'. He also commented on the 'hospitable little bar-parlour', and made the following remark about the publican, Arthur Hurn: 'Few men speak the Queen's English more beautifully, but this is not surprising in one who for many years travelled the world and swam in the full tide of human affairs'. He noted that 'In the bar-parlour there formerly stood polo-sticks of Dartmoor's beloved Prince, but war-time theft caused the remnant to be removed'. The postman at the time was William Withycombe, who had worked as a tin miner,[134] and who delivered mail on his ancient Raleigh bicycle.[135]

The stable accommodation housed five horses. It was situated on the opposite side of the road eastwards towards Bawden's (King's Oven) Bungalow. Bracken for their bedding was cut at Golden Dagger and stored in a barn there. There was also a milking cow called George (!) who would get taken down to Runnage Farm to be serviced, and a few geese were kept.

They also had a sheepdog called Kim.

Interior of the Warren House Inn, *c.* 1950 (*E. A. Sweetman & Son Ltd* – Stanbrook collection)

Moses Bawden's Bungalow/King's Oven Bungalow, east of the Warren House Inn (SX 67538107) in 1976. Built as a miners' dwelling *c.*1875, demolished by Dartmoor National Park Authority as a 'disfigurement' in 1976.

(*T. Greeves*)

David Hurn recalled how rabbits were an important source of income for him as a boy. He would get 6d a rabbit sold to Bill Oldreive of Headland Warren who had a contract to supply a fox farm near Widecombe. David could get a dozen rabbits slung across his pony's neck.

One moonlit night, David had the unfortunate luck of being caught ferreting for rabbits by Jim Endacott (c. 1889 -1974), the Duchy Reeve! A hand was suddenly placed upon his shoulder and he had to abandon his pursuit. He was escorted back to the inn where he had the idea of inviting Jim Endacott in for a drink to evade trouble. This apparently worked!

David Hurn also told how his father introduced red grouse onto different parts of Dartmoor. He would accompany his father and help release them.

Licensing hours were 10 a.m. - 3 p.m. and 6 p.m. - 9 p.m. William Younger's beer was delivered in wooden barrels or casks by lorry from Plymouth. Cider came from Inch's, and spirits were also sold. Water came from a spring on the east side of the inn. Dick Rowe, the baker from Chagford, delivered bread and fancy cakes. Esso Lube oil was also available, as well as petrol in two-gallon cans at 11d per gallon.

Two people who were then employed at the inn were Fernley Warne and Eddie Whiteway. Fernley was known as 'Swifty' because he was so slow when handling a broom, and Eddie was called 'Wasum' because his common response to a comment was: 'Wasum?'

'Silvertop' - Harry Warne at the Warren House Inn, 1920s (J. Weston - courtesy P. Parsons)

Harry Warne, tin
miner at Golden
Dagger Mine, late
1920s
(*D. Smith?* - courtesy
P. Sinclair)

Another character was 'Silvertop' (Harry) Warne who used to tell 'yarns' in the inn in return for free beer! 'Silvertop' was a well-known figure in the Warren House Inn, right up to the time of his death in 1942 at the age of sixty-four.[136] He was a tin miner from boyhood until the close of Golden Dagger Mine in 1930. He used to impress visitors to the inn with a bunch of white heather in his jacket pocket. When asked if he would sell it he would say 'no', but would eventually be persuaded to part with it in return for a drink. As soon as the visitors had left another bunch would be brought out - it is said that he used to blanch purple heather by placing boxes over it! He sometimes wore a smock and top hat.[137] 'Silvertop' is immortalised in at least two paintings by Dymond of the interior of the Warren House Inn showing a man sitting by the famous peat fire, which were reproduced and sold as postcards. One of the paintings shows him sitting in front of the fire with his two terrier dogs, Peter (left) and Paddy (right).[138]

Frequent visitors to the Warren House Inn included John Skittery, the Chief Constable of Plymouth (who had a house in Postbridge) and 'Rasher' Bacon, the 18-stone Chief Constable of Devon. He used to wear white shorts, much to the amusement of Mark Loram, a road contractor and pig dealer who was another frequent visitor. A well-to-do-couple, Charles and Peggy Clapham, used to drive to the inn every Sunday night in a Rolls Royce from Torquay. A lengthsman called Perryman was also a regular drinker.

Painting of Harry Warne inside the Warren House Inn, c. 1935, by R. J. Dymond, with dogs Peter and Paddy (*Charles Worcester & Co.* Stanbrook collection)

The advent of the motor car and coaches increased trade, and the inn would cater for coach parties by using the Tea Room on the other side of the road. However, no cooked food was served to the public.

Occasional lodgers were still taken in, usually friends, and they ate in the kitchen with the rest of the family where there was a 3-burner paraffin stove. A hut, just west of the garage which was attached to the inn, would provide sleeping accommodation for two extra visitors.

Unwelcome guests were three escapees from the Borstal at Dartmoor Prison. They broke into the inn via the sitting-room window in March 1946 and fastened the staircase door, thus locking the family in. They then stole David Hurn's naval duffel coat, clothing coupons, cheque books and cash, leaving orange peel strewn on the floor![139]

The Warren House Inn *c.* 1950, showing Tea Room opposite (*E.A. Sweetman* – Stanbrook collection)

The Warren House Inn in deep snow, 1928 (?) (*J. Weston*? - courtesy R. Petherick)

Group outside the Warren House Inn *c.* 1944 (left to right, identified by D. Hurn): Walter Rice of Moorgate, roadman; Walter Coppin of Postbridge, retired banker; American officer from the Claims Commission; American serviceman, name unknown; Mark Loram: unknown; unknown; Bill Withycombe in his Home Guard uniform; Arthur Hurn, landlord (photographer n/k – courtesy D. Hurn)

Group outside the Warren House Inn with Arthur Hurn third from left,
c. 1950 (photographer n/k – Greeves collection)

Severe winter weather was recorded early in 1939. The inn was cut off for at least a week. The *Western Morning News* published a photograph on 31 January of Joan Hurn on horseback, with food supplies. Another photograph of Joan Hurn on horseback appeared on 1 February 1939 in *The Daily Telegraph & Morning Post* revealing that she had ridden 10 miles for provisions.

The Hurns were at the Warren House Inn during the Second World War. Although relatively safe from enemy action, danger seemed closer to hand! In 1942, military training in the area of the inn resulted in pieces of shrapnel hitting the roof! A Ministry of Agriculture survey of 1941 noted the following livestock: 1 cow and heifer in milk; 1 cow in calf; 1 female cow 1 yr and under 2; 30 fowls over 6 months; 30 fowls under 6 months; 3 horses.[140]

Sydney Nicholls (b.1928) recalled walking to the inn from Grendon Farm with his uncle Wilf Irish in about 1945, across Soussons Down before any trees were planted, and picking their way between the mine workings of Golden Dagger and Vitifer. He sometimes had to hold onto his uncle's coat, for safety - in the dark![141]

In 1947 the inn was cut off for six weeks by snow and ice.[142]

MODERN TIMES (SINCE THE 1950s)

Just east of the Warren House Inn in January 1963 - Bawden's Bungalow in background (photographer n/k – Stanbrook collection)

In about 1955 the Hurn family was succeeded by Brian Sillem who came from South Creaber, Gidleigh and was known as 'Size Tens' - he is certainly remembered as having very large feet! He used to wear a Trilby hat.[143] His wife Madge was with him. He drove a left-hand-drive jeep and his wife drove a Jaguar. The cars were kept in the double garage on the west side of the inn.

The Sillems were there in the great winter of 1962/3 and photographs of the deep snow can be seen inside the Warren Inn today. Colin Endacott recalls that he and his father took a tractor from Jurston with provisions up to the inn once a 45-ton bulldozer had cleared a path, a week after the storm. They had to take an indirect route to Beetor Cross and then along the main road. By Bennetts Cross, as they approached the inn, they were driving through a 'tunnel' of snow with walls well over six feet (1.8m) high. Within these drifts it was sheltered; beyond there was the bitterest wind. Apart from the bulldozer driver, they were the first people the Sillems had seen for a week. It had taken the bulldozer two days to cut a way out to the inn from Beetor Cross after a previous attempt by Bill Aggett with a smaller machine (JCB) had failed. A helicopter brought relief supplies to the inn. The first ordinary vehicle to get through was the van belonging to Charlie Hill, the baker of Chagford.[144]

Peter Hutchings rented Lakeland (1.5 miles to the north-east) from the Sillems. His father had farmed at Willandhead and used to take potatoes to Princetown and return with beer for the pub. Peter Hutchings had to ride out daily through the snow from Lakeland on a Welsh cart mare, or walk if the snow had frozen hard, to milk the two South Devon cows which the Sillems kept in the stables across the road from the pub. They were large beasts and each needed ten gallons (45.5 litres) of water to drink per day. Peter Hutchings carried this in buckets from the inn. He came to appreciate how much a cow drinks! Mrs Sillem meanwhile had managed to break her thigh (femur) and was bed-bound downstairs in the sitting-room of the inn. When the huge quantities of snow began to thaw, there was nowhere for the water to drain and the inside of the pub flooded with water, drenching her bed.[145]

Mrs June Endacott of Jurston went to work for Brian and Madge Sillem soon after she was married in 1960. Her main task was to help in the Tea Room opposite the inn, which provided for coach parties (mostly Wallace Arnold), sometimes more than a dozen in a day. Inside there were tables with oilcloths. Crockery and a sink were at one end, with primitive kitchen facilities powered by gas cylinders. Dartmoor gifts were also sold here.

June Endacott used to milk the two South Devon cows. Clotted cream was made by Mrs Sillem, who also baked scones, and cooked meat to go inside sandwiches. Sponge cakes were baked by Mary Mortimore of Chagford. June Endacott was sometimes assisted by Mrs Ben Hutchings. She also helped behind the bar, and she and her husband used to look after the pub when the Sillems were away. June remembers one weekend of dismal weather when she saw nobody apart from Bob White the postman.

Local peat was still burnt in the fire in Brian Sillem's day - it was not the deep turf but the surface rooty material known locally as 'vags', each one of which measured about 12 x 7 x 1½ ins. Each vag would have to be cut and turned face down, dried, then turned face up, dried, then ridged into cloche shapes to allow the final drying by wind and sun. The vags would be cut in July or August and drying would take 5-6 weeks. They gave a distinctive and beautiful aroma, but were smoky and created a lot of dust. Inside the bar, pictures and all surfaces were stained brown from them. The Peat Room was on the east side of the building, against the famous fireplace gable. The last person to cut 'vags' for the pub was George Harvey of Lettaford (b. 1911), who recalled cutting 250 vags after school, when aged 8 or 9. When an adult, he was able to cut 100 vags in ten minutes. He remembers it as hard work, slicing the ground and pushing the 'vag iron' in front of him, and he made special pads for his hands. He would cut vags on Bush Down and near Chagford Cross (now Jurston Cross).[146]

Brian Sillem's opening hours were from 10 a.m. - 3 p.m. and from 7 p.m. - 9.30 p.m. His best beer was Bass kept in wooden barrels. A Start-o-Matic generator provided enough electricity for lighting, and cooking was done by means of gas cylinders. Among regular customers were Chris Hill from Lettaford, Mark Loram, and Jack Neck from Moretonhampstead. Every weekend Jack Neck would walk the moor or go fishing all day long. His brother Harvey also drank at the inn. About 18-20 people could squeeze into the single room, with standing room in the corridor. Beer was served through a small hatch which had a blind on which the opening hours were written.[147]

Interior of the Warren House Inn and its famous east fireplace, after changes of the mid- 1960s
(*K. Ruth* - Stanbrook collection)

Interior of the Warren House Inn (west fireplace) after changes of the mid-1960s (*K. Ruth* – Greeves collection)

Bill Ash as landlord, with Maurice Greenway as resident manager, took over during 1963 and made the major alterations which have created the present-day pub, opening up the whole of the downstairs, and exposing the original fireplace. The work was done by Jack Piper (b.1915) from Buckfastleigh, plus Wilf, a skilled mason and carpenter from Cornwall. Jack Piper and Bill Ash had a fudge-making business on Kilworthy Hill in Tavistock, with outlets in Mevagissey and Padstow. The renovation work at the Warren House Inn was done mostly in the winter, over a period of years. The second porch was demolished and replaced by a window. The Tea Room was also removed, despite occasional intensive use by coaches on the way to Cornwall. The garage was turned into a gift shop for a while. Eric Hext and Roy Mortimore from Chagford were employed on Sunday mornings to do maintenance work.

Maurice Greenway kept a link with the Prince of Wales public house in Princetown[148] and had been head waiter at the Two Bridges Hotel. He had aquiline features. A fine photograph of him was published in the *Western Morning News* of 4 February 1965. It shows him sitting in front of the famous fire, with two cats on his lap, and a dog (Rex) on the floor, talking to Jack Piper.[149] The owner of the leasehold at this time was a Lt-Col. D.C. Cocks.[150]

Ploughman's lunches, costing 2s 6d (12½p), were introduced for the first time. Harry Trude used to supply cabbage lettuces - he also carried on 'Silvertop's' practice of offering visitors 'white' heather, made by blanching purple heather under tins. It was Bill Ash who acquired the guns which used to hang on the walls. The new tables and bar top were of elm from the Dartington Hall estate, two inches thick, polished and varnished by Jack Piper.[151]

Dennis Seaman from Barnstaple was next to take over as landlord. He had a number of pubs. He employed Basil Goad, also from Barnstaple, as manager from 1969.[152] Harry Trude, a former tin miner at Golden Dagger and Vitifer, was employed as a handyman, and lived in the Warren House Inn with his wife Kitty in 1968. [153]

Basil Goad himself took charge in 1971, and stayed for thirteen years. A curious incident of a disappearing Pickfords pantechnicon happened during his occupancy. One foggy night two men parked the vehicle at right angles to the road, on the north side, with the front facing into the road. When they came to leave, rather the worse for drink, there was no sign of their truck. They assumed it had been stolen. The police were called and the pub was cleared. The drivers themselves were then arrested and taken to Tavistock where they spent the night in custody. In the morning they were returned to the scene of the 'crime' to discover that the truck had rolled across the road and down the slope, but miraculously had remained upright, although invisible in the night-time fog. Eventually it was winched out and found to have sustained no significant damage![154] In August 1975 the *Western Morning News* reported a chimney fire which required attendance by the fire brigade, who doused the fire but fortunately failed to douse the smouldering peat in the famous fireplace itself. It was claimed then that 100 tons of logs were burned in the fire each year.[155]

In December 1984 Tony Berry from Croydon took over. He had a pub near Bridport in Dorset, and moved to Derbyshire when he left the Warren House Inn. He was followed by Peter Parsons, who bought the lease from him in 1988, though he had

Peter and Janet Parsons, August 2001 (*T. Greeves*)

actually first worked in the Warren House Inn for one season in 1976, returning in 1982-3. Peter, who was the son of the landlord of the Three Crowns in Chagford, has remained at the Warren House Inn since, with his wife Janet, and two sons James and Jonathon. During his time he has built a new generator shed and provided an air-conditioned cellar which prevents freezing of beer and tonic water in the pipes, and the 'waxing' of gas due to the cold. He has also built on a new room, behind the old ever-burning fireplace. Water comes from a spring - occasionally the supply runs short due to increasing consumption of water (in both kitchen and home).

In 2001, he reckoned to burn at least 40-50 tons of logs (supplied by Jason Thomas) in the two fires each year, at a cost of about £50 per week. Among long-term staff he has employed are Dave Cooper (grandson of tin miner Jack Warne), Roger Evans, Angela Gourlay, Joss Hibbs, Darren Owen, Dan Sharland, Colin Smerdon and Jenny White.

Peter reckons the foot-and-mouth epidemic of 2001 was the most difficult period he has had to cope with. His busiest period was the day of the total eclipse of the sun on 11 August 2000 - he opened at 9 a.m. and was packed all day, with cars parked on both sides of the road, right to the horizon. On 'millennium eve', 31 December 1999, he lit a beacon in a brazier on the other side of the road, and a very good time was had by many of his regular customers. He prides himself on running a 'traditional' pub with real ale, local scrumpy and good food (including 'warreners' rabbit pie' and a range of vegetarian dishes), locally sourced wherever possible.

Apart from the 'serious cold' that can be experienced, wind can also cause problems - in the late 1990s three young people in a camper van parked outside, had a meal in the pub and returned to their van to brew some tea. They put up the roof of the van, whereupon it was caught by a gust of wind, and blew right into the field below the tables. Luckily, it was undamaged, but the occupants inside were very shaken. Peter himself sold ice creams from a caravan for a time, and this, too, was blown right across the road. Flooding by rainwater up to a foot (30 cm) deep is another occupational hazard.[156]

The present inn sign shows three rabbits following each other in a circle and cleverly sharing three ears between them. During the 20th century this symbol came to be labelled erroneously as 'the tinners' rabbits'. It is in fact a pre-Christian symbol of hares, with the oldest known examples occurring in Buddhist China in about AD 600.[157] However, in its rabbit form it is highly appropriate for an inn of which the name commemorates a rabbit warren. Basil Goad had a metal sign showing three rabbits, but Peter Parsons replaced it in the early 1990s with the painted version used today. The earlier sign for the inn showed a single rabbit. This was provided by John Weston of north London who got an artist friend to design it. The Weston family regularly took holidays on Dartmoor, and John Weston was a keen photographer.[159]

The Warren House Inn is an occasional location for filming of advertisements or television programmes. Tom Baker, as 'Dr Who' was filmed among the mining remains at Vitifer in the 1970s. In the early 1980s the brewery Mann & Co. renamed the pub the George & Dragon and covered its west elevation with plastic ivy.[159] In 2000, part of an episode of 'The Bill' was filmed here for television.

The Mid-Devon Hunt meeting outside the Warren House Inn, 20 January 2001 (*T. Greeves*)

The inn is still a meeting point for local hunts - historically the South Devon met here.[160] Today, both the Mid-Devon and South Devon meet here from time to time.

Since this book was first published in 2001, Peter and Janet Parsons have continued to run the pub. The major change to the Warren House Inn has been the opening in June 2009 of the new dining room on the east side of the property. This had previously been used to store peat 'vags' for the fire and was where the outside toilets had once been located. It was later used as a cellar room (for storing beer) and at the back it housed a generator. After a new generator shed had been built outside, as well as a refrigerated cellar at the back of the building, preparations and work began in the spring of 1991 (!). New windows were inserted, and access made through to the public bar, bar and kitchen. Over a succession of winters electrics were fitted, flooring, heating and a bar were installed, and repointing of walls took place, besides building and staining of the settles. Much of the work was initiated by William Tyler, father of Janet Parsons, as well as her brother Rodney. The final push over a couple of months saw completion of the room and the hanging of a collection of framed photographs of the pub in the 1920s, taken by Mr J.Weston and kindly given to the Parsons family by his daughter the late Peggie Wallace (many of the pictures are reproduced in the book). A 'jumper', a classic stonecutter's tool, now hangs on a wall, having been donated by David Cooper.

There have inevitably been staff changes. Helen Gay, Ryan Taylor and Emily Taylor have been longstanding employees. Marc and Andrew Smerdon, Jonathan Martin and Cedar Shaw all started work in the pub at the age of thirteen and now return from university to work during holidays. Jamie and Jonny Parsons also now work in the pub during holidays from school. Dickon Perryman is a new young recruit. Wood for the famous fire is now sourced from Tavistock.

Peter Parsons behind the bar of the Warren House Inn (*E. Stanbrook*)

To step inside this 'free house' with its burning fires on a wild winter night is to enter a snug and atmospheric world. Outside, at any time of year, the sound of the generator, the smell of wood smoke, or the invigorating damp aroma of the unique cocktail of heather, bracken and peat, will alert the visitor to the remarkable moorland setting of this pub. In August the purple heather is in flower. The view (except in fog!) is spectacular. Almost a mile away, slightly north of east, is the rocky outcrop of Birch Tor at 1593 ft (485m). Due east, over the extensive tinworking gullies and beyond the first heathery ridge, can just be made out the grey walls of the famous prehistoric enclosure known as Grimspound. To the south-east a conspicuous stone wall running east-west down the hillslope is the parish boundary between Manaton and North Bovey. A granite-walled enclosure can be seen on the slope of Birch Tor and another to the south - these are two of four in the area built with rabbit-proof walls. Their last usage was as a source of emergency winter feed for rabbits - they were planted with gorse and broom and the rabbits only had access when deep snow had obliterated their normal food supply - heather. More romantically, they are said to represent the four aces in a pack of cards, dropped by the wicked Jan Reynolds who had made a compact with the Devil, who grabbed him from his pew in Widecombe church on 21 October 1638 amidst a terrible storm which caused death and destruction.[161] To the south lies Soussons Plantation - a coniferous woodland planted in the late 1940s. Six miles away to the south-east a prominent rock outcrop can be spied - it is Buckland Beacon from which there are spectacular views. South-westwards in the middle distance are the plantations of Bellever Forest, with the high southern moor on the far horizon.

This is the story of the Warren House Inn so far. There is no reason why its future should not be as interesting and as varied as its past. We, the authors of this booklet, will be pleased to hear from any reader who has memories or photographs which can add to the tale.

APPENDIX OF KNOWN PUBLICANS

New House

1786	William Tapper
1815-1823	Robert Browning (Moreton Inn)
1824-1826	James Jenkin (Moreton Inn)
1827-1828	William Honey/Huns (Moreton Inn)
1834-1845	Jonas Coaker

Warren House Inn

1845	Jonas Coaker ?
1850-1851	Joseph Warne
1857	William Jinnings
1861	William Maddock
1863-1882	Joseph Warne
1883-*c.*1920	Thomas and Elizabeth Hext
1921-1929	William Stephens
1929	Mary Stephens
1930-*c.*1955	Arthur Hurn
c. 1955-1963	Brian Sillem
1963-1968	Bill Ash and Maurice Greenway
1968-1971	Dennis Seaman
1971-1984	Basil Goad
1984-1988	Tony Berry
1988-	Peter Parsons

REFERENCES

1. A list of English inns reputedly higher in altitude than the Warren House Inn was published in *Dartmoor Magazine*, **103**, Summer 2011, 67.
2. Greeves, 1995.
3. D(evon) R(ecord) O(ffice) 1292M/Drafts/Lydford/2
4. DRO/QS/63/3/12/001; 63/5/01/049; 63/6/09/100; *Exeter Flying Post* 23.9.1841/3B; Crossing, 1912, 265.
5. Crossing, 1912, 329.
6. Greeves, 1986, 21.
7. Groves, 1970, 194-6.
8. Donn, 1765, Sheet 6B.
9. Ravenhill, 1965, 8.
10. Moore & Birkett, 1890, 88-90; Spooner & Russell, 1953, 333.
11. Du(chy of) Co(rnwall) London, Dartmore Proceedings 1735-1777/309, 5.12.1737.
12. Moore & Birkett, 1890, 22.
13. Rowe, 1896, 303.
14. DRO/36652/P1.
15. Somers Cocks, 1970, 98.
16. Moore & Birkett, 1890, 11.
17. idem, 21.
18. idem, 23, 26-7, 33, 36-7.
19. idem, 38-9.
20. idem, 89.
21. Newman, 2002; 2011, Fig. 8.12, p.153.
22. Greeves, 1986, 25.
23. DRO/1429A/PW2.
24. DuCo London/Dartmoor Applications for Grants etc from Messrs Carpenter, Frazer & Cole 1789-1793/16.3.1791.
25. Greeves, 1986.
26. Brown, M., 1999, Vol.40 p.2.
27. Gough, 1789 (1806 edn), 48.
28. Raistrick, 1967, 21.
29. Gray & Rowe, 2000, 38.
30. Svedenstierna, 1804, 29.
31. DuCo London/Bundle - Miscellaneous 1807-12, 1.2.1817, Amies to Gray.
32. F.Hodge, taped interview 29.12.1972.
33. DRO/Z17/3/8, p.28, Wm Simpson's Survey of the Forest of Dartmoor.
34. DRO/QS 62/7A/1-32.
35. Batten & Bennett, 1996.

36. DRO/QS 62/7A/1-32.
37. Wood & Tapley-Soper, 1938.
38. idem.
39. DRO/QS 62/7A/1-32; 63/4/02/015; 63/5/08/016.
40. Lydford Parish Registers.
41. DRO/QS 63/6/05/017; 63/7/01/003.
42. Wood & Tapley-Soper, 1938.
43. idem.
44. Lydford Parish Registers.
45. Bray, 1836, **1**, 294-7; see also Bellamy, 1998, 113 for a remark about the 'ancient' status of New House in 1851.
46. Crossing, 1911, 68-9; 1912, 250-1; see also Tickler, 1873, 46, whose slightly different version of the rhyme inserts a first line: 'John Roberts lives here'.
47. Pigot, 1830, 209.
48. DRO/924B/B8/30-31.
49. Bray, 1836, **1**, 27-33.
50. Fitch, 2000.
51. Brown, T., 1961, 19.
52. DuCo Princetown/Letters Sent 22.4.1870.
53. DRO/Z 17/2/9.
54. *Woolmer's Exeter & Plymouth Gazette,* 9 Sept 1843.
55. inf. M. Stephens.
56. Greeves, 1992.
57. Baring-Gould, 1896, 150-1; Wright, 1896, 99-100; Crossing, 1912, 475.
58. Burnard, 1889-90, 195-6.
59. DuCo Princetown/Letters Sent 22.4.1870.
60. DRO/DP 148.
61. Bray, 1836, **1**, 296-7.
62. C.Warne, noted conversation 19.7.1984.
63. Baring-Gould, 1896, 149.
64. Rowe, 1848, 126.
65. *Mining Journal,* 2.2.1850, p.54; 9.2.1850, p.64; 16.2.1850, p.63.
66. DuCo London/Box 59/8.10.1851.
67. White, 1850, 803; Bellamy, 1998, 113.
68. Baring-Gould, 1908 (1926 edn). Second Series, 298-9.
69. DRO, Widecombe Parish Registers.
70. Billings, 1857.
71. DuCo Princetown/Letters Sent 23.10.1858.
72. idem, 4.2.1860.
73. Crossing, 1912, 244.
74. Census Return 1861.
75. DuCo London/ Letters Sent 2.8.1860-1.12.1862.
76. *Tavistock Gazette*, 8.5.1863.

77. Census Return 1871.
78. White 1850; Morris 1870.
79. C.Hill, noted conversation 12.5.1975.
80. DRO,Widecombe Parish Registers.
81. *Kelly Mine Preservation Society Newsletter*, June 2000; A.Woodley 17.8.2001.
82. DuCo Princetown; inf. Bob Cowan.
83. Woods, 1996, xi.
84. MS notes by R.Burnard in bound volume: Six-Inch OS Map of Dartmoor Vol. I/Sheets XCIX NE & XCIX SE; Crossing, 1912, 251.
85. Crossing, 1911,30.
86. DuCo Princetown/Letters Received 1.2.1869.
87. idem/Letters Sent 2.2.1870.
88. idem/Letters Received 3.2.1875.
89. Murray, 1887, 201.
90. F.Willcocks, noted conversation 25.2.2001.
91. Widecombe Parish Registers.
92. J.Hamlyn, noted conversation 31.5.1985; email from Paul Hext 12.4.2011.
93. Greeves, 1986, 38; email from Paul Hext 12.4.2011.
94. DuCo Princetown/Letters Received 1897.
95. DuCo London/Box 59.
96. J.Endacott, noted conversation 6.12.1973.
97. C.Hill, noted conversation 12.5.1975; email from Paul Hext 12.4.2011.
98. Greeves, 1986, 38; F.Hodge, taped interview29.12.1972; Hemery, 1983, 511.
99. F. Hodge, taped interview 29.12.1972; S.French, noted conversation 7.11.1974.
100. J.Endacott, noted conversation 6.12.1973.
101. Mrs W.Webb, noted conversation 23.8.1972; W.Warren, noted conversation 31.8.1972.
102. F.Webber, noted conversation 7.5.1974; Crossing, 1911, 30.
103. W. Bennett, noted conversation 13.3.1974.
104. Census Return 1891.
105. Census 1901.
106. J.Leaman, noted conversation 15.4.1976.
107. C.Hill, noted conversation 4.11.1977.
108. DuCo Princetown, letter 21.7.1904.
109. Greeves, 1986, 41; Mrs G.Prew, noted conversation 3.10.1984.
110. Mrs G. Prew, noted conversation 26.7,1984; Census 1911.
111. Mrs E.Bellamy, noted conversation 18.7.1976.
112. Greenstreet, 1996.
113. Letters in *Dartmoor Magazine*, **45**, 25 and **46**, 12.
114. P(ublic) R(ecord) O(ffice)/IR 58/ 66262.
115. DuCo Princetown, letter 29.1.1912.
116. Private papers.
117. Private papers.
118. Mrs V.Cole, noted conversation 15.8.1985.
119. Mrs B.Brook, noted conversation 19.9.2000.

120. R.Wills, *in litt.*7.7.1996.
121. Census Return 1911; G.Austin, noted conversation 20.10.1981.
122. Private papers.
123. Private papers.
124. K.Williams, noted conversation 19.6.1986.
125. A.Irish, noted conversation 30.5.2001; *Totnes Times*, 1929.
126. F.G.Warne, noted conversations 5.10.1993; 7.12.1993.
127. W.Flewin, noted conversation 1.7.1996.
128. *Devon & Exeter Gazette*, 26.3.1929; *Totnes Times*, 1929.
129. Private papers.
130. Mrs M.Wallace, noted conversation 3.2.1996; *Western Times*, 10 Jan 1930.
131. D.Smith, noted conversation 17.3.1992.
132. Private papers.
133. Private papers.
134. Greeves, 1986.
135. Westcountry Studies Library, Exeter/Dartmoor Collections/Hamlyn Parsons Vol.1.
136. *Western Morning News*, 30 Dec 1942.
137. J.Rawlins, noted conversation 30.4.2001.
138. Postcards published by C.Worcester.
139. *Western Times*, 8 March 1946; D.Hurn, noted conversation 10.1.2000.
140. PRO/MAF 32/679/351.
141. S.Nicholls, noted conversation 12.4.2001.
142. Brown, T., 1961, 19.
143. Grumley-Grennan & Hardy, 2000, 72-3.
144. C. & Mrs J. Endacott, noted conversation 23.4.2001; P. Hutchings, noted conversations, 14.5.2001 and 18.5.2001.
145. P.Hutchings, noted conversation 18.5.2001.
146. P.Hutchings, noted conversation 18.5.2001; G.Harvey, noted conversation 8.8.2001.
147. P.Hutchings, noted conversation 18.5.2001; D. McMaster, *in litt.* 23.4.2002
148. Electoral Registers 1963 and 1964.
149. *Western Morning News* 4.2.1965; G.Grose, in litt. 9.7.2001.
150. *Western Morning News* 13.2.1965.
151. Postcard sent 27.4.1965 (Stanbrook collection); J.Piper, noted conversation 30.8.2001.
152. Electoral Register.
153. Electoral Register.
154. P. Hutchings, noted conversation 18.5.2001.
155. *Western Morning News* 9.8.1975.
156. P.Parsons, noted conversation 2.8.2001; Hedges, 1999.
157. Greeves, 1991; 2000; 2001.
158. Mrs M. Wallace, noted conversation 3.2.1996.
159. *Dartmoor Magazine*, **12**, 2.
160. Tozer, 1916, 306 etc; Hemery, 1983, 518, plate 258.
161. J. Hamlyn, noted conversation 31.3.1983; Crossing, 1912, 249, 318.

BIBLIOGRAPHY

Baring-Gould, S. (1896) *Dartmoor Idylls* (London)

Baring-Gould, S. (1908) *Devonshire Characters and Strange Events* (London, 1926 edn)

Batten, K. & Bennett, F. (1996) *The Printed Maps of Devon - County Maps 1575-1837* (Devon Books, Tiverton)

Bellamy, R. (1998) *Postbridge - The Heart of Dartmoor* (Devon Books/Halsgrove, Tiverton)

Billing, M. (1857) *Directory & Gazetteer of the County of Devon...* (Birmingham)

Bray, A.E. (1836) *A Description of the Part of Devonshire Bordering on the Tamar and the Tavy...* (3 vols, London)

Brown, M. (1999) *Dartmoor Field Guides* (Dartmoor Press, Plymouth)

Brown, T. (1961) 'Tales of a Dartmoor Village - Some Preliminary Notes on the Folklore of Postbridge', *Trans. Devon Assoc.*, **93**, 194-227

Burnard, R. (1889-90) 'Jonas Coaker, the Dartmoor Poet', *Western Antiquary*, **9**, July 1889-June 1890, 195-6

Crossing, W. (1911) *Folk Rhymes of Devon* (Exeter and London)

Crossing, W. (1912) *Guide to Dartmoor* (Plymouth, 2nd edn)

Donn, B. (1765) *A Map of the County of Devon*

Fitch, T. (2000) 'The Salted Corpse', *Dartmoor Magazine*, **58**, Spring 2000, 30-31

Gill, C. (ed.) (1970) *Dartmoor - A New Study* (David & Charles, Newton Abbot)

Gough, R., ed. (1789) *Britannia... by W. Camden* (2nd edn, 1806)

Gray, T. & Rowe, M., eds (2000) *Travels in Georgian Devon - The Illustrated Journals of the Reverend John Swete (1789-1800)*, Vol.4 (Devon Books/Halsgrove, Tiverton)

Greenstreet, A. (1996) 'A Dartmoor Birth', *Dartmoor Magazine*, **44**, Autumn 1996, 20-21

Greeves, T. (1986) *Tin Mines & Miners of Dartmoor - A Photographic Record* (Devon Books, Exeter)

Greeves, T. (1991) 'The Tinners' Rabbits - Chasing Hares?', *Dartmoor Magazine*, **25**, Winter 1991, 4-6

Greeves, T. (1992) 'The Bellever Tor Hunt 1875 - A "New" Poem by Jonas Coaker', *Dartmoor Magazine*, **27**, Summer 1992, 5-7

Greeves, T. (1995) 'King Arthur's Oven - Dartmoor's First Tourist Attraction?', *Dartmoor Magazine*, **39**, Summer 1995, 6-8

Greeves, T. (2000) 'The Three Hares - Dartmoor's Ancient Archetype', *Dartmoor Magazine*, **61**, Winter 2000, 8-10

Greeves, T. (2001) 'Three Hares - A Medieval Mongol Mystery', *Devon Today*, April 2001, 58-63

Groves, R. (1970) 'Roads and Tracks' in Gill, C. (ed.) *Dartmoor - A New Study* (David & Charles, Newton Abbot, 182-203

Grumley-Grennan, T. & Hardy, M. (2000) *Gidleigh - A Dartmoor Village Past and Present* (Glebe Publishing, Gidleigh)

Hedges, M. (1999) 'Life at the Warren House Inn', *The Dartmoor Society Newsletter*, **4**, February 1999, 4-8

Hemery, E. (1983) *High Dartmoor - Land and People* (Robert Hale, London)

Kelly, E. R. (ed.) (1866) *The Post Office Directory of Devonshire*

Moore, S.A. & Birkett, P. (1890) *A Short History of the Rights of Common upon the Forest of Dartmoor & the Commons of Devon* (Dartmoor Preservation Association Publications No. l, Plymouth)

Morris & Co. (1870) *Commercial Directory and Gazetteer of Devonshire*

Murray, J. (1887) *A Handbook for Travellers in Devonshire* (London, 10th edn, revised)

Newman, P. (2002) *Headland Warren and the Birch Tor and Vitifer Tin Mines* (Archaeological Investigation Report Series A1/34,2002, English Heritage, Swindon)

Newman, P. (2011) *The Field Archaeology of Dartmoor* (English Heritage, Swindon)

Pigot, J. & Co. (1830) *National Commercial Directory* (London)

Raistrick, A. (ed.) (1967) *The Hatchett Diary - A Tour Through the Counties of England and Scotland in 1796* (Bradford Barton, Truro)

Ravenhill, W. (1965) 'Introduction' in *Benjamin Donn - A Map of the County of Devon 1765* (facsimile edn, Devon & Cornwall Record Society & The University of Exeter), 1-20

Rowe, S. (1848) *A Perambulation of the Antient & Royal Forest of Dartmoor & the Venville Precincts* (Plymouth)

Rowe, J. B. (ed.) (1896) *A Perambulation of the Antient & Royal Forest of Dartmoor...* (Exeter and London, 3rd edn, revised)

Somers Cocks, J. (1970) 'Saxon and Early Medieval Times' in Gill, C. (ed.) *Dartmoor - A New Study*, 76-9

Svedenstierna, E. (1804) *Tour of Great Britain 1802-3* (trans. E. Dellow, David & Charles, Newton Abbot, 1973)

'Tickler' [E.Tozer] (1873) *Devonshire Sketches - Dartmoor and Its Borders* (Exeter, 3rd edn)

Tozer, E. (1916) *The South Devon Hunt* (Teignmouth)

Wood, E. & Tapley-Soper, H. (eds) (1938) *The Register of Marriages, Baptisms and Burials of the Parish of Widecombe-in-the-Moor, Devon* (Devon & Cornwall Record Society, Exeter)

Woods, S. (1996) *Widecombe-in-the-Moor - A Pictorial History of the Dartmoor Village* (Devon Books, Tiverton)

Wright, W. (ed) (1896) *West Country Poets - Their Lives and Works* (London)

ACKNOWLEDGEMENTS

We are indebted to the staff of the Devon Record Office, Exeter; of the Westcountry Studies Library, Exeter; of the Public Record Office (now The National Archives), London; and of the Duchy of Cornwall Offices in London and Princetown, for access to their records. We also thank the Courtauld Institute for permission to use material from their photographic archive. We are specially grateful to Peter and Janet Parsons of the Warren House Inn for their help, interest and loan of photographs. Many of those who generously provided information are listed in the references. Warm thanks are due to these and specially to Mr R. Bellamy, Mrs B. Brook, Mr D. Cooper, Mr R. Cowan, Mr & Mrs C. Endacott, Mr G. Grose, Mr G. Harrison, Mr G. Harvey, Mr P. Hext, Mr D. Hurn, Mr P. Hutchings, Mr B. Le Messurier, Miss A. Mortimore, Mr S. Nicholls, Mr N. Parkhouse, Mr R. Petherick, Mr J. Piper, Sir J. Rawlins, Mr K. Ruth, Mr P. Sinclair, Mr M. Stephens, Mr S. Taylor, Mr R. Wills and Mr A. Woodley.

INDEX